THIS WALKER BOOK BELONGS TO:

_____

_____

_____

_____

For Paul and Adam

First published 1988 by Walker Books Ltd
87 Vauxhall Walk, London SE11 5HJ

This edition published 1998

4 6 8 10 9 7 5 3

© 1988, 1998 Shirley Hughes

Printed in Hong Kong

British Library Cataloguing in Publication Data
A catalogue record for this book is
available from the British Library.
ISBN 0-7445-4983-3 (hb)
ISBN 0-7445-6062-4 (pb)

Out and About

through the year

Shirley Hughes

WALKER BOOKS

AND SUBSIDIARIES

LONDON • BOSTON • SYDNEY

Out and About

Shiny boots,
Brand new,
Pale shoots
Poking through.
In the garden,
Out and about,
Run down the path,
Scamper and shout.
Wild white washing
Waves at the sky,
The birds are busy
And so am I.

Mudlarks

I like mud.
The slippy, sloppy, squelchy kind,

The slap-it-into-pies kind.

Stir it up in puddles,
Slither and slide.

I *do* like mud.

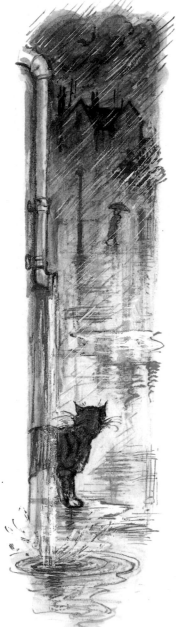

Wet

Dark clouds,
Rain again,
Rivers on the
Misted pane.
Wet umbrellas
In the street,
Running noses,
Damp feet.

Spring Greens

Bulbs in pots,

Twigs in jars,

Dads in the street, washing cars.

Greens in season,

Trees in bud,

Sky in puddles,

Ripples in mud.

Birds in bushes, singing loud,

Sun tucked up in a bed of cloud.

Water

I like water.
The shallow, splashy, paddly kind,
The hold-on-tight-it's-deep kind.

Slosh it out of buckets,
Spray it all around.

I *do* like water.

Squirting Rainbows

Bare legs,
Bare toes,
Paddling pool,
Garden hose.
Daisies sprinkled
In the grass,
Dandelions
Bold as brass.
Squirting rainbows,
Sunbeam flashes,
Backyards full
Of shrieks and splashes!

Sunshine at Bedtime

Streets full of blossom,
Like pink and white snow,
Beds full of tulips,
Tucked up in a row.

Trees full of "candles"
Alight in the park,
Sunshine at bedtime,
Why isn't it dark?

Yet high in the sky
I saw the moon,
Pale as a ghost
In the afternoon.

Hill

Huge clouds
Slowly pass;
Huge hill
Made of grass.
Jungle under,
Thick and green,
Tangled stalks –
Creep between;
Scramble up,
Hug the ground...

Suddenly see
All around!
Watch out, fences,
Fields and town!
From the top of the world
I come rolling down.

Sand

I like sand.
The run-between-your-fingers kind,
The build-it-into-castles kind.
Mountains of sand meeting the sky,
Flat sand, going on for ever,
I *do* like sand.

Seaside

Sand in the sandwiches,
Sand in the tea,
Flat, wet sand running
Down to the sea.
Pools full of seaweed,
Shells and stones,
Damp bathing suits
And ice-cream cones.

Waves pouring in
To a sand-castle moat.
Mend the defences!
Now we're afloat!
Water's for splashing,
Sand is for play,
A day by the sea
Is the best kind of day.

The Grass House

The grass house
Is my private place.
Nobody can see me
In the grass house.
Feathery plumes
Meet over my head.
Down here,
In the green, there are:
Seeds
Weeds
Stalks
Pods
And tiny little flowers.

Only the cat
And some busy, hurrying ants
Know where my grass house is.

Feasts

Apples heaped on market barrows,
Juicy plums and stripy marrows.

Grains of barley,
Carefully stored,

Feasts of berries,

Nuts to hoard,

And ripe pumpkins, yellow and green,
To light with candles at Hallowe'en.

Wind

I like the wind.
The soft, summery, gentle kind,
The gusty, blustery, fierce kind.
Ballooning out the curtains,
Blowing things about,
Wild and wilful everywhere.
I *do* like the wind.

Misty

Mist in the morning,
Raw and nippy,
Leaves on the pavement,
Wet and slippy.
Sun on fire
Behind the trees,
Muddy boots,
Muddy knees.

Shop windows,
Lighted early,
Soaking grass,
Dewy, pcarly.
Red, lemon,
Orange and brown,
Silently, softly,
The leaves float down.

Sick

Hot, cross, aching head,
Prickly, tickly, itchy bed.
Piles of books and toys and puzzles
Heavy on my feet,
Pillows thrown all anyhow,
Wrinkles in the sheet.
Sick of medicine, lemonade,
Soup spooned from a cup.
When will I be *better*?
When can I *get up*?

Fire

Fire is a dragon
(Better beware),
Dangerous and beautiful
(Better take care).
Puffing out smoke
As soon as it's lit,
Licking up leaves,
Crackle and spit!

Sending up sparks
Into the sky
That hover a moment
And suddenly die.
Fire is a dragon,
Alive in the night;
Fiery dragon,
Glittering bright.

Hoping

Grey day,
Dark at four,
Hurry home,
Shut the door.
Think of a time
When there will be
Decorations
On a tree,
Tangerines,
And hot mince pies,
A bulging stocking,
A Christmas surprise!

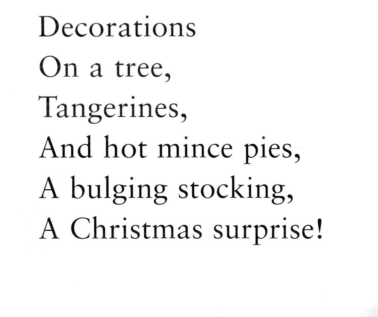

Cold

Cold fingers,
Cold toes,
Pink sky,
Pink nose.
Hard ground,
Bare trees,
Branches crack,
Puddles freeze.
Frost white,
Sun red,
Warm room,
Warm bed.

MORE WALKER PAPERBACKS
For You to Enjoy

Also by Shirley Hughes

THE NURSERY COLLECTION

Colours, shapes and sizes, sounds, opposites and numbers –
these are the concepts introduced to young children in this delightful nursery picture book,
which features a lively toddler and her equally engaging baby brother.

"Predictably first class… Concepts are introduced with domestic examples and
Hughes' characteristic gentle humour." *The Guardian*

0-7445-4378-9   £6.99

TALES FROM TROTTER STREET

"All the ingredients for a good story – humour, attention to detail, a few anxious moments,
a home truth or two and a bit of a lump in the throat…
Excellent and recommended for 4 – 7 year-olds and all their families."
Books for Keeps

0-7445-2032-0   *Angel Mae*
0-7445-2033-9   *The Big Concrete Lorry*
0-7445-2012-6   *Wheels*
0-7445-2357-5   *The Snow Lady*

£4.99 each

UP AND DOING

Each of the books in this series for pre-school children takes a single everyday verb and
shows entertainingly some of its many meanings and applications.

"There's so much to look at, so much to read in these books."
Children's Books of the Year

0-7445-3652-9   *Bouncing*
0-7445-3654-5   *Chatting*
0-7445-3653-7   *Giving*
0-7445-3655-3   *Hiding*

£4.50 each

Walker Paperbacks are available from most booksellers, or by post from B.B.C.S., P.O. Box 941, Hull, North Humberside HU1 3YQ

24 hour telephone credit card line 01482 224626

To order, send: Title, author, ISBN number and price for each book ordered, your full name and address,
cheque or postal order payable to BBCS for the total amount and allow the following for postage and packing:
UK and BFPO: £1.00 for the first book, and 50p for each additional book to a maximum of £3.50.
Overseas and Eire: £2.00 for the first book, £1.00 for the second and 50p for each additional book.

Prices and availability are subject to change without notice.